CONTENTS

PREHISTORIC BEESTON

ENGLISH HERITAGE

ABOVE *Flint arrowheads of the Neolithic period. The right-hand one is broken at the point*

BELOW *Bronze Age axe found at Beeston. The hollow socket in the head of the axe was fixed on to a wooden or bone handle and secured by leather thongs passed through the loop and tied round the shaft*

ENGLISH HERITAGE

ENGLISH HERITAGE (CHRIS EVANS)

Loom weights made of baked clay were found in the Iron Age settlement on the hill. The weights would have been attached to the vertical warp threads of the loom, keeping them taut and allowing horizontal strands to be woven through to form the cloth

EARLY SETTLERS

Although apparently isolated, Beeston crag is part of a chain of hills stretching across Cheshire from north to south. This higher ground was more easily cleared than the badly drained and marshy lowland areas, so in earlier times it was used for travel, for cultivation and for settlement.

Beeston was long thought to be a possible settlement site, but it is only very recently that archaeological excavations have proved the matter beyond doubt. Remains have been found of a Bronze Age community living here about 800BC. One of the community was a skilled smith who made tools and weapons in bronze.

Excavations have also shown that about four hundred years later the hill slopes were again in use, this time fortified by a bank and ditch across the part most vulnerable to attack. Protected by these defences, an Iron Age settlement flourished here. Its members grew corn and kept sheep, and lived in timber framed huts which were probably round in shape with conical roofs.

Some of the finds from the excavations are in the exhibition at the castle entrance.

FROM HILL FORT TO CASTLE

The hill fort was abandoned probably by the beginning of the Roman period. A few tantalising Roman finds have come from the base of the hill, near the present entrance, as well as the hint of a Roman road, but during the period of Roman rule and during the centuries that followed, Beeston's history is obscure.

It emerges from the shadows again when Ranulf, sixth Earl of Chester, and one of the most powerful lords of his time, chose the crag as the site of his new castle.

BUTSER ANCIENT FARM PROJECT TRUST

Reconstruction of an Iron Age hut, built on the site of the Butser Ancient Farm Project, Petersfield, Hampshire

ENGLISH HERITAGE (CHRIS EVANS)

Roman brooch of the second century AD, found on the lower part of the hill

RIGHT *Beeston Crag from the west*

EARL RANULF'S CASTLE

Crusaders attacking the walls of the Egyptian town of Damietta

RANULF THE CRUSADER

Ranulf was born in 1170, the only son of Hugh, fifth Earl of Chester. He became the sixth earl on the death of his father in 1181 and inherited one of the richest earldoms in the kingdom, with estates spreading across England from Cheshire to Lincolnshire. In 1188 he married Constance of Brittany, widow of the king's son, Geoffrey Plantagenet, and so, through marriage, became related to the kings of England.

The seal of Ranulf, sixth Earl of Chester. One side shows the Earl on horseback and in armour; the other, his coat of arms, three wheatsheaves. The inscription reads 'The seal of Ranulf, earl of Chester and Lincoln'

Ranulf was both a warrior and a statesman. For several years he countered the guerrilla warfare of the Welsh with his own raids into North Wales, but in 1218 he entered into an alliance with his former enemy, the Welsh ruler Llewellyn ap Iorwerth ('Llewellyn the Great') and brought peace to Cheshire. In the same year he set out on a pilgrimage to Jerusalem, but on the journey there was persuaded to join the Fifth Crusade and, sailing to Egypt with other warriors, took part in the siege of Damietta, a town near the mouth of the Nile, then held by Saracens. The town was captured in November 1219.

Ranulf returned to England in 1220 and five years later began to build his castle at Beeston.

THE CASTLE OF THE ROCK

Ranulf's principal castle in Cheshire was at Chester where he had his residence, his law courts and his treasury. Why, then, build a new castle just fifteen miles away?

There are three possible reasons. Firstly, a change in the king's advisers had left Ranulf less influential and less secure than hitherto. Secondly, new ideas in castle building gave the opportunity to build a different and more sophisticated type of castle. Thirdly, the crag at Beeston was an ideal site to put these new ideas into practice. So Ranulf set about the creation of an impregnable stronghold not just for security but also as a symbol of his power and importance.

He planned the castle in two parts. On the top of the crag he cut a great ditch through the rock to create the Inner Bailey, a relatively small enclosure which, with its walls, towers and gatehouse, and with precipitous cliffs on three sides, was the most secure part of the castle.

On the lower slopes he created the Outer Bailey whose walls and towers followed the contours of the ground and which had another massive gatehouse, fronted by a ditch, at its entrance.

The defences were carefully planned and skilfully arranged, using the natural strength of the site to its maximum advantage. In medieval documents Beeston is referred to as *Castellum de Rupe*, the 'Castle of the Rock'. It is a vivid and accurate description.

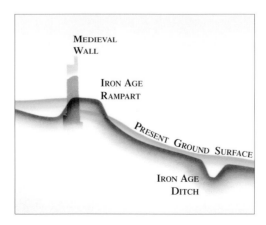

The medieval castle wall stands on the site of the Iron Age rampart. The drawing shows the position of castle wall, Iron Age rampart and ditch, and the present ground surface

4

CASTLE DESIGN

Castle design was constantly changing. In the twelfth century the most prominent part of many castles was a huge tower or 'keep'. It was usually surrounded by other defences but the ultimate strength of the castle sprang from the massiveness of this one dominating tower, its height, and the thickness of its walls. Should the other defences be over-run, the tower could still hold out.

There is no such tower at Beeston. Instead, two new devices were used to withstand attack. Firstly, the surrounding walls were built with a series of small projecting towers which allowed defenders

in an English castle at Orford Castle in Suffolk in the 1160s, and the beginnings of a powerful gatehouse are to be seen at Dover Castle, dating from the 1180s. However, the importance of Beeston is that for the first time the strength of the forti fications rested entirely on these two features. For the first time also the gate-house appeared in a fully developed form, capable of playing a major role in the defence of the castle. It is the forerunner of the formidable gatehouses of Edward I's great castles in North Wales, built at the end of the thirteenth century.

Who designed the Beeston defences? Almost certainly it was Earl Ranulf himself. He was one of the foremost military leaders

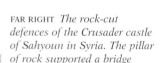

Rhuddlan Castle, North Wales. Built between 1227 and 1282 on the orders of Edward I, its two great gatehouses are direct descendants of those at Beeston

FAR RIGHT *The rock-cut defences of the Crusader castle of Sahyoun in Syria. The pillar of rock supported a bridge*

RIGHT *The Inner Ditch at Beeston*

to fire across the faces of the walls and sweep away any attacking force. Also, because the towers were higher than the walls, the garrison was able to control the walls on either side as well as the bank and ditch in front. By these means the castle wall became not just a passive barrier but the most important line of defence.

The second innovation is the provision of powerful gatehouses at each entrance. At earlier castles the entrance was simply a gateway in the wall, or in a tower. At Beeston, the two gatehouses are the strongest parts of the castle and important elements in its defence.

Neither of these devices was entirely new. Wall towers were first used systematically

of his time, experienced in warfare, and fully informed about the latest methods of fortification. He had no need to look outside England to obtain the ideas for his new castle. Nevertheless, he was in Egypt for two years, rubbing shoulders with fellow Crusaders and hearing at first hand of the castles in Syria and the Holy Land with their sophisticated defences, their hill-top sites, and their vast rock-cut ditches. For a man of Ranulf's intelligence and experience it did not need a great leap of the imagination to picture the crag at Beeston as the place for a stronghold of the same type and with the same power and magnificence. He lived to see his new castle taking shape, but not to see it completed.

BELOW *Two iron keys and a belt or strap buckle found during excavations at the castle*

5

A ROYAL CASTLE

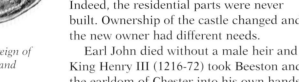

A gold penny from the reign of Henry III, King of England

KING HENRY III

The castle was unfinished at Ranulf's death in 1232, and still incomplete at the death of his successor, John, the seventh earl, in 1237. Most of the defences had been built by this time but there were no permanent living quarters other than the chambers in the gatehouses and in some of the towers. Indeed, the residential parts were never built. Ownership of the castle changed and the new owner had different needs.

Earl John died without a male heir and King Henry III (1216-72) took Beeston and the earldom of Chester into his own hands. The earldom had become too important, and Beeston too powerful, to be outside the king's control, especially at a time when trouble was threatening from Wales.

WAR AND WALES

The brief period of peace in Cheshire and North Wales brought about by Ranulf's alliance with Llewellyn in 1218 was followed by more than sixty years of intermittent warfare. King Henry's use for Beeston was mainly as a base to assemble troops and supplies for his campaigns against the Welsh, and as a place to keep prisoners and hostages. He did not need it as a residence so no attempt was made to equip it with the halls and chambers, kitchens and storerooms seen in other castles of comparable size. It remained simply a fortified enclosure with a small, permanent garrison which lived, probably, in timber buildings in the Outer Bailey.

In 1254 Henry gave Beeston, together with all the other castles and lands of the County of Chester, to his eldest son Prince Edward, the future King Edward I. Edward was also given the title Earl of Chester which, from that time, has always been granted to the eldest son of the sovereign of England.

BELOW *Thirteenth-century masons at work cutting stones, raising materials with a treadmill crane, and laying stones to build a wall*

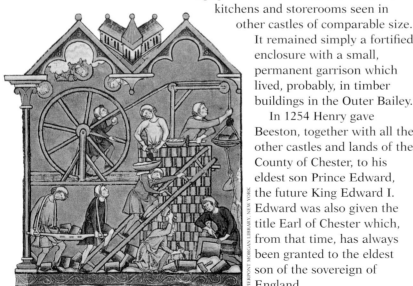

IMPROVEMENTS AND REPAIRS

Edward was crowned king of England in 1272 and in two campaigns completed the conquest of Wales. With North Wales pacified, the Cheshire castles lost some of their importance, but Beeston was kept in good repair and, indeed, strengthened. In 1303/4, major works were put in hand and details of the work are known from accounts kept by the king's officials.

Carpenters were paid for obtaining timber from Delamere Forest and for using it to repair three towers in the Inner Bailey. They also cut planks, made a scaffold, built 'machines' for raising the timber (probably a windlass or a treadmill crane), and made new steps, doors, windows, 'galleries', and a new bridge. The master carpenter in charge of the work is named as Hugh de Dymoke and the expenditure for the year amounted to just over £23. Other payments were made for carting the timber from the forest, including payments to the men in charge of the oxen which pulled the carts.

Master Warin was in charge of the masons working at the castle. They worked on three towers in the Inner Bailey, increasing their height and building battlements. They also built a new stone ramp in front of the gatehouse.

The cost of the masons, and the wages of a smith and his assistant for making and sharpening tools and for making other ironwork ('large hinges, hooks, and great locks and keys for the great gate, and for the doors and windows of the three towers') amounted to £38. This included the cost of making a forge for the smith at the castle, and payments to women for carrying water.

Other items were payments to 'Roger le Belgeter' for supplying 22lbs of brass, for iron, steel and coals, for ropes, and for soap and grease for the 'machines'. Jordan de Bradeford and Benedict de Staundon were paid for lead needed for the new roofs of the towers and 'Thomas le Plumer', a monk at Combermere Abbey (near Malpas), was paid for working the lead into sheets. 'Madoc le Quarreour' supplied lime which was bought at Chester and carted to Beeston to make lime mortar for use in the new stonework.

ENGLISH HERITAGE (IVAN LAPPER)

The sums of money spent on the building works may seem absurdly small. Consider, however, that in 1285 masons, carpenters, and smiths were paid two shillings and sixpence (12.5p) for a week's work, and that a labourer was paid at most one shilling (5p) per week, and it will be seen that, translated into modern values, the total expenditure was considerable.

NEGLECT AND DECAY

During the fourteenth century the castle was kept in good repair, but thereafter the story is one of gradual decline. By the sixteenth century Beeston was of no further use to the Crown. It was acquired by a local landowner, Sir Hugh Beeston of Beeston Hall, who allowed some of the poorer members of his family to live in part of the castle and use the land for farming.

Little thought was given to military requirements. The defences were neglected and parts of the walls collapsed. In 1642, however, domestic peace was rudely shattered by the outbreak of the Civil War and the castle was hastily brought back into use.

ABOVE *The stone ramp shown here in reconstruction in front of the Inner Bailey gatehouse was built in 1303-4. Payments to stonemasons for work on the ramp are recorded in building accounts. Part of the ramp still survives under the modern bridge. Before the ramp was built, the ditch was spanned by a timber bridge, whose framework rested on a central pillar of rock which is still visible in one side of the ramp*

BELOW *Iron nails found in the Inner Ditch near the ramp*

ENGLISH HERITAGE

BELOW *Monument to Sir George Beeston in Bunbury Church, near Beeston. Sir George commanded the 'Dreadnought' against the Armada in 1588. He died in 1601, aged 102. His son, Sir Hugh Beeston, was the owner of the castle at the beginning of the seventeenth century*

CHESTER CITY RECORD OFFICE

7

PRINCE EDWARD AT BEESTON

AN ILLUSTRATION by Ivan Lapper of the castle as it might have appeared on 13 August 1265. After the battle of Evesham on 4 August 1265 and the defeat of Simon de Montfort, Earl of Leicester, and the rebel barons, Prince Edward rode north with his knights and men-at-arms to seize his Cheshire castles from Simon's supporters. He entered Beeston without opposition and while there heard that Chester had surrendered.

One of Simon's supporters, Humphrey de Bohun, son of the Earl of Hereford, was wounded and captured at Worcester. He was taken to Beeston and died there from his wounds on 27 October 1265.

The painting shows the Inner Bailey with a timber palisade on its north side, and depicts the type of buildings the garrison may have had in the Outer Bailey. Edward's men-at-arms are camped in the grounds. On the far side of the Outer Bailey the castle wall is shown without towers. Very probably it had several, but the wall is now entirely destroyed and nothing is known of their positions or number.

Sir William Brereton, commander of the Parliamentary troops in Cheshire. A vigorous and successful leader, he was the son of William Brereton of Handforth, Cheshire, and was twice Member of Parliament for the county

ABOVE *During excavations at Beeston, a number of small iron plates were found which came from a type of jacket known as a 'jack of plates'. It is made of canvas, reinforced in the body and arms with overlapping iron plates sewn between two layers of canvas. Worn by soldiers in the sixteenth century, this type of armoured jacket was somewhat old-fashioned by the time of the Civil War, but no doubt provided effective protection for its wearer during the siege of the castle*

RIGHT *Nineteenth-century engraving of King Charles I addressing his troops at Wellington, near Shrewsbury, in September 1642*

THE CIVIL WAR

EARLY SKIRMISHING

On 22 August 1642 King Charles I raised the Royal Standard in Nottingham. The Civil War between Royalists and Parliamentarians had begun.

Although the decisive battles in the Civil War were fought on open ground, many old and dilapidated castles were repaired and garrisoned and subsequently proved their strength by withstanding prolonged sieges. Beeston was one of these.

The first troops to seize the castle on 20 February 1643 were Parliamentarians, acting on the orders of their commander in Cheshire, Sir William Brereton. He 'caused the Breaches to be made up with mud-walls, the Well of the outer Ward to be cleansed, and a few rooms erected'. This done, the Parliamentary garrison settled in. The local Royalist headquarters were in Chester, a place of great importance to King Charles as the main port for troops and supplies from Ireland.

The summer and autumn of 1643 passed by with relatively little action in Cheshire, but in November part of the royal army in Ireland landed in Chester. On the morning of 13 December 1643, after the moon had set but before dawn, Captain Thomas

Sandford of the army from Ireland with eight men got into Beeston Castle 'by a byeway through treachery, as was supposed' and persuaded the Parliamentary garrison of sixty men, commanded by Captain Thomas Steele, to surrender.

It is believed that Sandford and his eight men scaled the precipitous cliffs on the north side of the castle and gained entry into the Inner Bailey, but exactly how and where they slipped into the castle is not known.

Steele, outwitted by the smaller but more determined Royalist force, led his men out of the castle and back to the Parliamentary headquarters in Nantwich. He was tried and shot for his conduct.

THE SIEGE

For eleven months the Royalist garrison in the castle was largely untroubled, but in November 1644 Brereton's troops laid siege to both Beeston and Chester. At Beeston they rounded up cattle from near the castle, fought off a Royalist attempt to recover them, and positioned troops in nearby farms to prevent all access.

The Royalist reply was vigorous.

ABOVE *A burial against the north wall of the Inner Bailey. Two skeletons have been found in this area, and although neither can be dated with certainty they may belong to the Civil War period*

LEFT *Seventeenth-century glass window In the parish church of Farndon, Cheshire. The paintings are of Royalist soldiers of Sir Francis Gamul's Regiment in the King's army at Chester. The four central panels depict weapons and armour commonly used in the Civil War*

On 7 December, forty to fifty men slipped out of the castle, surprised twenty-six Parliamentarians dining in a house at the foot of the hill, set fire to the house and killed all but two of its occupants.

The siege was lifted on two occasions and the garrison's supplies replenished, but it was resumed immediately the relieving forces moved away. To make the siege more effective Brereton's men dug a trench round the foot of the hill and built a fortified position or 'mount', capable of holding a hundred men, opposite the Outer Gatehouse.

By November 1645 the Royalist garrison was starving. Terms of surrender were agreed and near midnight on 16 November its commander, Captain Vallett, came out with his men, drums beating and flags flying. According to one seventeenth-century writer 'Theire was neither meate, Ale nor Beere, found in the Castle, save onelie a peece of a Turkey pye, Twoe Bisketts, a lyve Peacock and a peahen'.

The city of Chester surrendered on 3 February 1646 and the first part of the Civil War ended later that year with King Charles I a prisoner of the Scots.

A WORK OF MERCY

To the worshipful Committee or the Several Justices of Peace, whom this may concern.

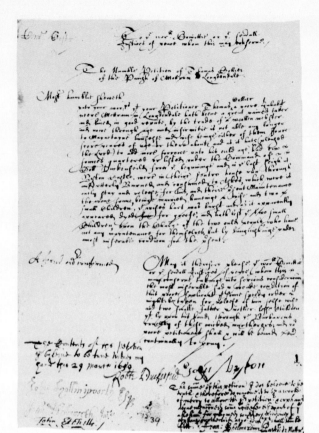

The Humble Petition of Thomas Collier of the Parish of Mottram in Longdendale.

Most humbly showeth unto your Worships that your Petitioner Thomas Collier a poor inhabitant near Mottram in Longdendale has been a great pains taker and lived in good repute, by the trade of a woollen webster [weaver], and now through age and infirmity is not able any longer to maintain himself and wife being either of them four score years of age or thereabouts and as it has pleased the Lord to add more sorrow unto his old age, had two sons quartered or listed under the Command of Col Dukenfield from the beginning, and in the last siege at Beeston Castle, were in their sentry house run through and utterly burned and consumed to ashes, which were the only stay and relief for him and their present maintenance the one son, being married, having a wife and two small children, the wife's heart was burst and as it apparently appeared died for grief, and has left the two small children upon the charge of the two old people who have not any maintenance for themselves but lie languishing under most miserable conditions for the present.

May I therefore please the worshipful Committee or the Several Justices of Peace, whom this may concern, taking into serious consideration the most miserable sad and weak condition of this poor suppliant that some speedy order might be taken for relief of himself, wife and two small father and mother-less children that lie upon his hands through the barbarous cruelty of those wicked murders; and your petitioner shall and will be bound over continually to pray.

ABOVE *The petition of Thomas Collier of Mottram-in-Longdendale in north-east Cheshire, to Justices of the Peace, for money to support the petitioner and his wife in old age, and the two orphaned children of one of his sons. The petition describes how Collier's two sons were killed in the 'sentry house' during the siege of Beeston Castle, which is probably the incident of 7 December 1644 when 26 Parliamentary soldiers were trapped in a house near the castle and all but two were killed. It is typical of many petitions made after the war, which are a reminder of the loss and suffering caused by four years of fighting*

ENDORSED: *The contents of this petition I believe to be true my hand this 29 March 1650.*

Robert Dukenfeild

(Signed also by John Vryton, John Hollinworth, John Hollinworth Jnr and John Etchells)

ENDORSED: *The substance of this petition I do believe to be truth and therefore do conceive it to be a work of mercy to allow the said petitioner and orphans above mentioned some relief either out of the assessments for maimed soldiers widows and orphans or other wise as your worships shall think fit.*

Francis Shelmerdine, Pastor of Mottram

RIGHT *Seventeenth-century pots and dishes reconstructed from some of the thousands of broken pieces recovered during recent excavations at the castle. These vessels were probably used by the Civil War garrison*

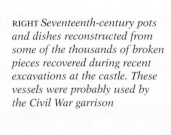

LATER HISTORY

South view of Beeston Castle, drawn and engraved by the Buck brothers in 1727

ENGLISH HERITAGE

A S BERESFORD

A S BERESFORD

CENTRE AND ABOVE *Visitors to the castle in about 1910 are shown in these old photographs*

At the end of the Civil War, orders were given for Beeston's defences to be destroyed. Not all was demolished, however, as you can see from the remains today, and in 1703 a tenant, George Walley, was renting and living in the 'castlegate', probably the Outer Gatehouse. By 1722 he had moved to a cottage on the east side of the hill

Ownership of the castle passed by marriage to Sir Thomas Mostyn of Mostyn Hall, Flintshire (Clwyd). The hill was let for grazing and quarried for stone. In 1722 there is a reference to a 'horse causeway' leading up to the castle, and probably about this time most of the Outer Gatehouse was pulled down to give better access to the quarries.

In 1840, the Beeston estate was purchased by John, 1st Lord Tollemache, member of Parliament for South Cheshire from 1841 to 1868 and later for West Cheshire. The quarrying for stone and sand continued, but what was left of the castle began to be valued as a picturesque ruin. Some repairs were carried out and in 1846 the present gatehouse was built at the entrance. Visitors were permitted to view the ruins and from about 1851 a fête in the grounds became an annual event. Deer were kept on the hill and, for a time, kangaroos. In 1897 Queen Victoria's Jubilee was celebrated with a bonfire, and in 1902 a special fête was held to mark the coronation of King Edward VII.

BELOW *Three items dropped by visitors to the castle:* TOP *nineteenth-century bronze eyepiece from a telescope;* RIGHT *eighteenth-century ornament from a walking stick;* LEFT *bronze fob with an inset topaz (nineteenth-century)*

ENGLISH HERITAGE

13

TOUR OF THE CASTLE

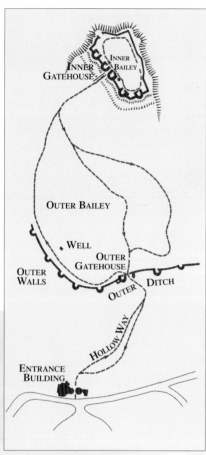

FROM ENTRANCE TO OUTER GATEHOUSE

The **Entrance Building** to the castle grounds is the work of the first Lord Tollemache in 1846. He was the first to appreciate the value of the ruins and to open the castle to visitors. The modern extension was made in 1979 to house an exhibition.

From here to the castle there is a choice of route. Either take the 'hollow way' which is forward and then to the right; or climb the slope on the right and walk along the upper path. Both lead to the Outer Gatehouse of the castle.

The 'hollow way' was made in the eighteenth century to get stone and sand from the quarries within the castle. It is referred to in 1722 as the 'horse causeway'.

The **Outer Gatehouse** and castle wall were begun in 1225 by Ranulf, Earl of Chester. Much of the gatehouse has been destroyed, but originally it had a central entrance passage between two large D-shaped towers.

On either side are the high walls of the castle, standing above a steep bank. Below the bank are the remains of the Outer Ditch. It is clearly visible on the left-hand side of the track although, filled with earth and debris, it is only a shadow of its original size. It was, when fully cleared, 3m deep and 5m wide.

The right-hand ditch is both smaller and older. Although nowadays you can barely see its line, it was 2.5m deep and 3m wide and was part of the defences of an Iron Age hill fort. Archaeological excavation has also uncovered the remains of the rampart of the hill fort, made of boulders and stones reinforced with timber stakes. It was found under and in front of the castle wall.

As you pass through the gatehouse, notice the slot for the **portcullis** in the side wall. In the left-hand tower are the remains of a chamber which had a door and window in its back wall and, in its front wall, two wide openings each with an arrow slit. One slit pointed forwards, and the other sideways across the entrance. The outer tower of the gatehouse was arranged in the same way so that, firing through these slits, archers stationed in the towers could subject any attacker to a deadly hail of arrows.

ENGLISH HERITAGE (IVAN LAPPER)

LEFT *A reconstruction by Ivan Lapper of the Outer Gatehouse. Before destruction it was a large and forbidding building, three storeys high. The entrance passage was protected by a gate and portcullis, but there was no drawbridge. The high tower on the left is a later addition and was built with three small chambers, one above the other. The gatehouse was probably dismantled after the Civil War and further destroyed in the eighteenth century when a track was driven through to the stone and sand quarries inside the castle.*

BELOW *View of Beeston from the south. In the middle distance is the wall of the Outer Bailey. Lord Tollemache's entrance building is at the bottom of the hill.*

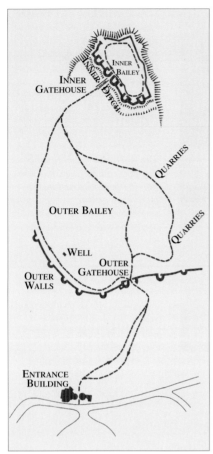

FROM OUTER GATEHOUSE TO INNER BAILEY

Beyond the gatehouse, follow the path to your left and walk along the inside of the castle wall.

Follow the wall as it curves towards the higher ground. It is 1.75m thick. Originally, it had a walk-way, protected by battlements, along the top, which make a fighting platform for the garrison to defend the walls, and gave access from one tower to another.

The **towers** are D-shaped in plan, two storeys high and open at the back. Only five towers survive but, originally, the wall continued up the hill to the Inner Ditch. The sites of more towers are visible as hummocks on the ground. A few paces from the fourth tower is a **Well.** It was still in use in the seventeenth century and at that time was 73m deep. Now it is choked with debris to within a short distance of the surface.

Within the walls is the **Outer Bailey.** It is as huge area, much larger than the garrison required, but when armies were on the move, needing overnight quarters and storage space, this part of the castle could easily accommodate the tents and shelters of a temporary encampment.

Continue up the hill but, before crossing the bridge to the Inner Bailey, pause at the **Inner Ditch.** This is entirely man-made, cut through the natural rock by the medieval masons. Stone from here was used as building material for the castle.

When first made, the ditch was spanned by a timber bridge, supported on a central pillar of rock. Later, this was replaced by a stone ramp which led to a drawbridge in front of the gatehouse. Remains of the ramp can be seen under the modern bridge, and in the left-hand side of the ramp is part of the rock pillar of the first bridge.

The **Gatehouse** has a central passage between D-shaped towers. As you walk through the passage notice the portcullis slot and the recess for a gate.

There are two chambers at ground floor level, one in each tower, and a single chamber on the floor above, extending across the central passage. Access to it was through an outside doorway in the back wall, reached probably by ladder. However, although it provided some accommodation, heated, if at all, by braziers, the gatehouse was designed primarily for defence. Its massive walls, its arrow slits in the ground floor chambers, and its fighting platform at roof level, made it a formidable obstacle to any attacker. The alteration and partial blocking of the arrow slits was probably done in the Civil War. Muskets had replaced bows and a different sort of opening was needed for these weapons.

RIGHT The entrance to the Inner Bailey. The remains of the medieval ramp can be seen below the modern bridge

The Outer Bailey well. When in use it probably had a windlass for raising water

Wall towers were important parts of the castle's defences. From their roofs archers controlled the banks and ditch in front of the walls and guarded the wall-walks on either side. From the ground-floor embrasures within the towers, other archers could fire across the front of the castle walls, exposing any attackers to cross-fire. The cutaways show an archer in action in one of the ground-floor embrasures. Above are steps leading to the wall-walk

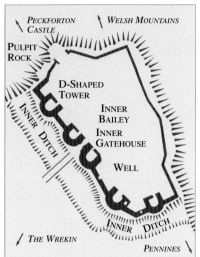

The map labels:
PECKFORTON CASTLE · WELSH MOUNTAINS · PULPIT ROCK · D-SHAPED TOWER · INNER BAILEY · INNER GATEHOUSE · WELL · INNER DITCH · THE WREKIN · PENNINES

BELOW *The Inner Bailey from the north side*

THE INNER BAILEY

The views from the **Inner Bailey** are spectacular. To the west are the Welsh mountains. To the east are the Pennines, and on a clear day one can see the Wrekin, 30 miles (48km) to the south-east.

With precipices on three sides, the ditch on the other, and with its high walls and towers, the Inner Bailey was intended to be impregnable. Here, Earl Ranulf planned to have his living quarters, but, though the rock was levelled in various places in preparation, these were never built.

Moving in a clockwise direction, you pass one of the **D-shaped Towers** and from near here there is a good view of Peckforton Castle, a country house built in the nineteenth century in the form of a castle by the first Lord Tollemache. Further on the wall has been destroyed at a point where the rock juts out above a sheer drop. It is known as '**Pulpit Rock**'.

Continue to the north-west corner where the castle wall turns at right-angles and runs along the north side of the Bailey. For much of its length it has lost all but a few courses of stone but it is clear there were no towers at this part. This section of wall may have been built at a later time, after 1280, in a simpler form than Ranulf intended.

On the east side of the Bailey is another D-shaped tower and then a length of wall that stands to its full height. Beyond this, near the gatehouse, is a **Well**, vital for the garrison in times of siege. It is 124m deep and is one of the deepest castle wells in the country.

RETURN ROUTE

Leaving the Inner Bailey, the path veers to the left and goes down through the centre of the Outer Bailey. It crosses an area used for fêtes since the nineteenth century. The ground is levelled in places.

Further to the east (left), the area was extensively quarried in the eighteenth and nineteenth centuries. Many of the mounds are heaps of quarry waste. Quarrying also destroyed the castle wall in this area. It survives only in a short section north of the Outer Gatehouse where there are two towers, one open at the back and one closed.

Go through the Outer Gatehouse and descend the track to the main entrance.

South of the entrance buildings is a series of **Caves** hollowed out of the rock by quarrying.

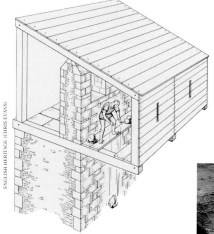

ABOVE *A 'hourd' or covered timber platform, built against the top of a castle wall as part of its defences. Beam holes for the timbers of a hourd survive in the wall of the Inner Bailey*

ABOVE *Part of the Inner Bailey, with the well in the foreground. Here the castle wall stands to its full height, and on its outer face are the beam holes for a hourd*

BELOW *The Beeston Caves*

19

The gatehouse of the Inner Bailey in about 1760, from a painting by George Barrett

FURTHER READING

The 'History of Cheshire', published by the Cheshire Community Council, is a good general history of the county, published in several parts. Three volumes are particularly useful for Beeston: B M C Husain, *Cheshire under the Norman Earls* (1973); H J Hewitt, *Cheshire Under the Three Edwards* (1967); and R N Dore, *The Civil Wars in Cheshire* (1966).

An excellent account of castle development in England is R Allen Brown's *English Castles* (3rd ed 1976). The best introduction to medieval building is L F Salzman's *Building in England down to 1540* (1952).

For the Crusades the three-volume *History of the Crusades* by S Runciman (1951-55) gives a detailed history. R C Smail, *Crusading Warfare 1097-1193* (1956) deals with fortifications as well as military campaigns.

M Ashley's *The English Civil War* (1974) is a concise general history of the period. R N Dore's 'Beeston Castle in the Civil War 1643-46' in the *Transactions of the Lancashire and Cheshire Antiquarian Society*, vols 75 and 76 (1965-66), is the most detailed account of the castle and Civil War siege.

The building accounts for work on the castle between 1301 and 1360 are printed in volume 59 of the Lancashire and Cheshire Record Society (1910), and the first report on the recent excavations at the castle is P R Hough's 'Excavations at Beeston Castle 1975-77' in *Journal of the Cheshire Archaeological Society*, vol 61 (1978). These excavations are discussed in full in *Beeston Castle, Cheshire* (ed Peter Ellis) English Heritage Archaeological Report no 23 (1993).

Musket balls found at Beeston, and a seventeenth-century pewter dish